Being the Medicine:
One Doctor's Reflection on his Medical Career

F. David Clifford, M.D.

Copyright © 2023 by F. David Clifford

All rights reserved.

ISBN: 9798376829455

Imprint: Independently published

Cover Design by Trevor Clifford

Dedicated to Lindsey Nell, PA-C, who exemplified to me being the medicine to her patients.

In adherence to the legal and ethical confidentiality guidelines defined in the Health Information Portability and Accountability Act (HIPAA), all unique identifiers of patients have been changed. Where possible, patients' written permissions for inclusion have been obtained.

CONTENTS

1	Introduction	1-2
2	One Friday in May	3-11
3	Vitamin E	12-14
4	Physician-Nurse Partnership	15-24
5	Tom said, "I think we loved each other too much."	25-26
6	A Complement of Mistaken Identity	27
7	Treating and Healing	28-33
8	Watch these Medical Providers in Action	34-36
9	Conclusion	37-38
	Notes	39-40

ACKNOWLEDGMENTS

Thanks to Diana Frazier, Amy Ordiway, Daniel Sastic and Chris Capitolo for their encouragement and corrections. Many thanks to Sam Hardman for his insights and guidance and my wife Diane for proofreading the text.

"I will remember that there is art to medicine as well as science, and that warmth, sympathy, and understanding may outweigh the surgeon's knife or the chemist's drug." Excerpt from Hippocratic Oath, modern version.

Chapter One
INTRODUCTION

This is part of the e-mail I sent to all my co-workers on my last day of work:

"**Family Medicine, done right, costs something.**
We enter into patients' pain, sorrows, joys, confusion, disappointment, all in the context of treating their diseases.
To be able to do that is difficult, but I would not trade it for the world!"

For 30 years I practiced primary care in rural northwestern Pennsylvania. After sampling the myriad options of medical specialties in medical school, I knew that family medicine primary care was what I wanted to do.

Primary care is defined as: "the provision of integrated, accessible health care services by clinicians that are accountable for addressing a large majority of personal health care needs, developing a sustained partnership with patients, and practicing within the context of family and community."[1]

This booklet is my distilling into a few paragraphs and thoughts what practicing Family Medicine meant to me. I offer it, as an expression of gratitude and as encouragement to the health care providers that continue to care for the most precious things on this earth, people.

Chapter Two
ONE FRIDAY IN MAY

Malcom James is a 57-year-old gentleman with diabetes. He is here today for a checkup. Malcom confesses that he "is not doing well." He is "experiencing something I never would have expected." Malcom's son and wife are splitting up. His son and children are now living with Malcom and his wife. This is stressing Malcom. He is not sleeping. Malcom expresses all this in his soft voice. His whole being exhibits quiet despair. He is lost.

I listen.
I look at Malcom's eyes.
I probe gently: "How are you handling all this? Is there an end in sight?"

My medical contract with Malcom obligates me to treat his diabetes. I am doing that. Malcom's son's marriage breakup affects his diabetes just as much as eating a chocolate fudge sundae for breakfast, lunch, and dinner for a week. There is no section of the evidence-based diabetes guidelines that addresses family discord. The guidelines urge me to measure Malcom's A1c (the average blood sugar level for the last 3 months) and tweak his meds to bring about gratifying, measurable results.

But today I choose the more arduous task. One that I cannot fix. And this is my first patient of the day!

I enter room 2 and sitting in chairs facing me are Jane Johnson and her husband. I sense a readiness for engagement in medical combat.

Jane's complaints are the same as last time. I know, because sometimes my notes quote the patient directly. Seeing a patient's identical quotes repeated in successive medical notes can mean one of two things: either that I have not fixed the problem, or it is a subtle testimony to my long-suffering labor. We had already investigated Jane's symptoms and obtained normal labs. Jane asks for the same labs today: thyroid, anemia, blood sugar. Could one of those things be abnormal and be causing her suffering?

Jane's husband is saying, "Something *has* to be wrong."

Jane's medical records show that her previous doctor had ordered appropriate tests – which were normal. (Why did she leave *that* doctor?) I affirm her symptoms and her suffering, but gently move her away from focusing on false causes with false solutions. It is easy to say, "All your tests are normal. I can't find anything wrong with you."

We all read about patients whose complaints were dismissed by many health care providers until one compassionate, diligent sleuth found the cause and delivered the person from a lifetime of pain. Is hers a case that only Sherlock Holmes, MD could crack? Am I too arrogant or lazy to look further? Am I doing enough to protect myself from a lawsuit in missing an obvious diagnosis? Is it right to send Jane to another consultant, when I really don't think they will find anything wrong? Am I being conscientious of medical dollars if I order some more expensive test?

I want to be the doctor she continues to make appointments with. But for the right reasons.

Robert Kingdom is a three-year-old with a painful right ear. He is wearing a shirt with a sequined robot on it. I rave about the robot and the sequins.

He devours the attention.

As I examine him, I discover he is wearing shark sneakers with a fin sticking up on the front of the shoe. I rave again!! The joy and innocence of wearing fun clothes.

I find a red tympanic membrane, and we get a chewable form of amoxicillin, because his mother says he does not take liquid antibiotics well.

I am replenished.

Fred Meyer is a 50-year-old with an accumulation of serious chronic medical diseases: diabetes mellitus, severe coronary artery disease and a CVA. (Cerebrovascular accident or stroke) Most recently, a catheterization showed terrible coronary arteries that cannot be stented or bypassed. One cardiologist stated, "There is nothing we can do." Meanwhile, Fred is having daily chest pain, relieved by multiple doses of nitroglycerin.

Fred is looking at his own mortality. There is a scared look just beyond his facial expression. He needs some affirmation, some support in his simmering desperation.

I come up with a trial of Lyrica, to address his daily chest pain. Can all his daily, frequent chest pain really be angina? I expound to him my theory that maybe his pain is from diabetic neuropathy (even though his diabetes is well-controlled). I give him Lyrica samples to try, telling him to get back to me, and we can increase the dose, if there is some relief.

I am not convinced that this is the answer, but it is an effort to acknowledge his need. And there is some science to it. When we have exhausted the guidelines and FDA-approved meds, is there nothing more we can do? There is always something you can do for a patient. It takes some creativity, diligence, sympathy, and thinking outside the box.

Jimmy Paris comes to me because his pulmonologist is retiring. Besides overseeing and prescribing Jimmy's CPAP for sleep apnea, the lung specialist also prescribed Ritalin for Jimmy's symptoms of daytime drowsiness. An earlier triage message had requested me to take over the prescription of Ritalin. Ritalin is a Schedule II stimulant under the Controlled Substances Act. I have decided to bring Jimmy in for an office visit to discuss the Ritalin issue.

In a face-to-face encounter for the purpose of deciding to prescribe Ritalin to an adult, I use my clinical-scientific skills along with my intuition and my personal knowledge of that patient. The classic paradigm of weighing benefits against risks applies both to the patient *and* to the prescriber. Ritalin is a medicine fraught with abuse, misuse, resale, and patient-doctor deception. There are layers of onerous legal, pharmaceutical, and insurance regulations the prescriber must wade through, to protect the patient and the provider against harm.

I ask Jimmy how long he has taken the Ritalin, and how it has helped him function. Jimmy is not well-versed on medical diagnostic jargon, but he does verbalize symptoms of inattention and improved concentration at work due to taking the medicine. Jimmy has a urine sample cup next to him. I agree to continue the Ritalin. I explain the protocols applied to Ritalin prescriptions. I ask him to give a urine sample, so we can screen for drugs. He is agreeable to everything.

Am I:

Going out on a limb?
Straying from the guidelines?
Being duped?
Adding to the "stimulant" crisis?
Trying to understand the patient and his life struggles?
Addressing his legacy[2] medication status?

Gray is more than a color. We should be courageous to function in that uncomfortable zone when it is appropriate.

Mercedes Gomez moved from Texas a few years ago. She lives with her daughter, who accompanies her to her office visit. Mercedes speaks Spanish, not English.

By now, we have established a routine: I address Mercedes in my halting, mangled, grammatically incorrect Spanish, which Mercedes hears, but often does not recognize as the language she speaks. Mercedes will spill out her Spanish words rapid fire, and I will frantically grasp a few key words. My non-verbal attentiveness and simple "*sí*" responses belie a lack of comprehension much of the time. I do speak English with Mercedes' daughter, to clarify symptoms, medication doses, blood tests, but I am very good at saying the numerical blood test results in Spanish.

Being from Texas, Mercedes is always cold in the Pennsylvania Siberia, which is northwestern Pennsylvania. At our last visit, I was kidding Mercedes for the multiple layers of clothing she was wearing. Today, I start with celebrating that fact that it is *"primavera"* (spring). Then I check how many layers of clothing she is wearing. We all laugh. Today I discover her *"calcitines con perros."* She is wearing socks with dogs on them!

I have learned that when you make the effort, though poor as it can be, to communicate with someone in their own language, they glow. You have won a friend.

This is the first visit for Louise Lancaster, an 81-year-old woman accompanied by her daughter, Sandy.

Sandy gives most of the medical history. Tucked in with the information about Louise's shoulder and orthopedic specialist is the declaration that "Mom has Alzheimer's."

My job today is to connect with Mrs. Lancaster. I place myself directly in front of her and look right into her face, asking her simple questions. My other job is to reassure her daughter that her beloved ward now is in the care of a doctor who understands and cares for her loved one.

I love being part of the special trinity of elderly parent, caring child, and doctor.

One of Sandy's requests, which often comes up in these settings, is whether we can cut back or remove some of Louise's multiple medications. Age, chronic diseases, specialists, and number of pills follow the same rising exponential curve. I feel only the smallest guilt, when I stop or lower a dose of some internist's prized pill. "First do no harm"[3] applies to culling redundant or ineffective meds from a confused, vulnerable elderly woman.

Brian L. Fitzgerald is a 47-year-old with diabetes mellitus, chronic anxiety, chronic insomnia, irritable bowel syndrome and chronic muscle pain. His symptoms persist despite two sleeping pills, an anti-anxiety pill, muscle relaxer, anti-depressant, and a neuromodulator.

He is a young curmudgeon. Today he relates a recent escapade in which he taunted the local police about ticketing cars parked against the direction of traffic. He admits to hating people. He is on probation at work and attends mandatory counselling.

Brian and I have found a topic of mutual interest. Brian has an encyclopedic knowledge of blues music. He cites and critiques specific artists and particular albums and has recommendations for my fledgling blues library. We also shared a penchant for Jerry Garcia ties.

Last Christmas Brian surprised me with a Jerry Garcia tie and a copy of <u>Presto: How I Made Over 100 Pounds Disappear and Other Magical Tales</u>. <u>Presto</u> is the book by Penn Gillete, the comedian-magician, in which he describes his potato diet. Brian wanted me to read the book and determine if he should follow it to lose weight.

I see 18 other patients that Friday. Most of those appointments fit into the mundane medical encounters that bring routine into the workday. They don't make exciting narratives, but they allow a doctor to go to the office for 37 years.

Chapter Three
VITAMIN E – ENCOURAGEMENT

Monday morning, I dispensed some encouragement to my flagging patients. Each had a different reason why they were running on empty in their daily struggle to keep their world in order.

Carolyn
Carolyn is being seen for a general checkup and refill of the stomach acid-reducer, pantoprazole. She has made a good recovery from a recent back surgery.

Carolyn expounds on her stress of caring for her husband with Alzheimer's dementia. She is living in an enclosed space with a man who careens from catatonia to hypermania. At one time she had summoned the police for protection and now if he gets too physical, she warns him, "I'll call the cops on you!" She says that in a light-hearted way in which one would threaten a mis-behaving child.

I let Carolyn describe the frustrating antics of her husband. "All he wants is sex and money, and he doesn't get either." We are roaring in laughter.

"He makes me play gin rummy with him every day."
"I hope you beat him," I said.
"Every day," she laughs.

Serious encouragement has to be delivered up close. My words have to be backed up with my eyes locked on the patient's. I am delivering an important message. I plant myself directly in front of Carolyn:

"You are *not* crazy"
"You are doing the *right* thing."
"You are the strong person"
"Don't believe the hurting words your ill husband says to you. Those are words spoken by the illness of dementia, which has possessed your loved one."

Randy
There are some patients who don't allow the nurse to weigh them because they can't face the number the scale assigns to them.

Randy is my beautiful 49-year-old bundle of nerves. She has a lifetime of struggling with her obesity. She is driving two hours to Cleveland as part of an Opti fast program. She has lost 12 pounds since starting the program two weeks ago.

Randy has anxiety and atrial fibrillation. Each of those maladies deliberately provokes the other. When her atrial fibrillation speeds up her heartrate, the palpitations ignite her anxiety. Her anxious adrenalin fires up her erratic atrial pacemakers.

Because her atrial fibrillation changed from being occasional to chronic, I sent Randy to a cardiologist for a consultation. Unfortunately, the specialist "first *did* some harm"[4] during his medical encounter with Randy.

"All he saw was my weight. When he described the ablation procedure to cure my atrial fib, he told me that I would not survive the procedure due to my weight. His only advice was for me to have a gastric bypass."

Randy continues, "That is the one thing I will not do. I know too many people who did poorly with gastric bypass." Randy wants reassurance that it was OK for her not to see that cardiologist again. I apologize for her mistreatment by the cardiologist and assure her that she is not going back. The expert on physical hearts bruised and battered her emotional heart.

Vitamin E has a synergistic effect when administered with lots of Vitamin A- Affirm, affirm, affirm.

Chapter Four
PHYSICIAN-NURSE PARTNERSHIP

The physician-nurse relationship can be defined as the professional interaction, co-operation, communication, and collaboration that exist between physicians and nurses. Collaboration is working with colleagues towards an agreed objective and is advanced through consultations with patients and colleagues.[5]

In Isaiah Baiyekusi's research, "Physician-nurse relationship: Nurses' perception in internal medicine and surgical units," he discusses the different types of physician-nurse relationships. The one deemed excellent was described as a collegial relationship.[6]

The core ingredient of collegial relationships is "different but equal" power and knowledge.[7] The collegial relationships are further characterized by equal trust, power, and respect. Physicians and nurses often regard themselves as peers or colleagues in describing these relationships.[8]

My delivery of medical care is done as part of a therapeutic partnership with nurses. Integral to "being the medicine" to our patients, nurses complement, correct, and catalyze my care. My nurses know my medical habits. They balance my tendency to fly by the seat of my pants with their accuracy and meticulous measuring and tying up loose ends. They laugh at my jokes and tolerate my crazy antics. The salutary effect of this professional duo is a prime example of the result being greater than the sum of its parts.

(The use of "my" when referring to the nurses I have worked with is not one of "possession." It is used in the same way I would expect nurses to refer to "my doctor." I use it to express a profound and treasured relationship.)

All needles don't have to hurt.

As a family physician, I have only a few "procedures" that I can resort to that will bring a robust insurance reimbursement or create an instantly gratifying "wow" response from a patient.

One such gratifying procedure is injecting a patient's painful greater trochanteric bursa. I am drawn to this steroid injection because the target is easily hit, unlike other arthrocentesis injections in which I must advance the needle through a narrow opening between two arthritic bones.

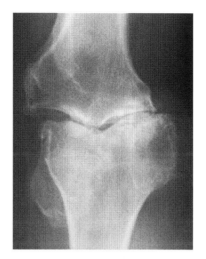

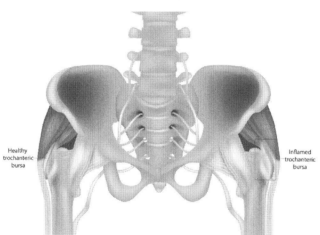

Morgan Faul, RN puts Mrs. Smith in the exam room. "Needs injection for a painful hip" is the reason for Mrs. Smith's visit. Morgan and I are excited about the chance to perform our Penn and Teller Injection Routine.

When I enter the exam room, Morgan has already prepared both the room and the patient. Procedure materials are laid out in operating suite neatness. Morgan's bright confidence is reassuring Mrs. Smith, who is anticipating being assaulted with a sharp object. The patient is lying on her side on the exam table, her left hip exposed.

I push on the skin overlying her greater trochanteric bursa. "Ouch! You hit the spot!"

Eliciting that tenderness on the first try is instilling some confidence that this doctor might just know what he is doing. I make an imprint in the skin with my fingernail. Morgan puts her index finger on the hip, pointing at the faint mark, while I turn to load up a gauze pad with betadine. While I am cleansing the target, Mrs. Smith says, "Make sure you use the good stuff." She has had this procedure before and knows the numbing pleasure of ethyl chloride spray. I spray the freezing liquid until a white frozen sheen covers the area.

"Make sure we are using the clean needle," I say to Morgan in a voice really meant for the patient's ears.

As I stretch a latex glove over my right hand, I complain, "I can't find any left-hand gloves," referring to the box of generic latex gloves that are made to fit either hand.

Poised with the needle above Mrs. Smith's orange painted hip, I reassure her with: "This won't hurt *me* a bit."

"All done."
"That didn't hurt a bit!"

Morgan applies a band aid and cleans up the betadine and helps to reassemble the patient and sit her up.

When Mrs. Smith walks down the hallway, she tests her hip and declares, "It's feeling better all ready." Another happy customer.

The Joanne Forsberg School of Remote Tropical Medicine, Lomalinda, Colombia.

In my first year of medical practice after completing my Family Medicine Residency, I took my young family to Colombia, South America for a three-month medical mission stint. Lomalinda was a self-sufficient missionary community located in the Llanos of Colombia. The Llanos are a tropical grassland plain east of the Andes Mountains. Two hundred inhabitants lived in simple homes scattered among little hills. The community included a school, hanger and airstrip, diesel power plant, commissary, language study offices. And a clinic.

Joanne Forsberg, the seasoned nurse who ran the clinic and provided medical care in the absence of any physician, pushed me into the deep end of the pool. Having been surrounded by specialists, senior physicians, state of the art imaging, laboratory results, and libraries, I was now the only medical doctor in charge of the health of 200 people isolated in the middle of Colombia. My urban residency program did not include casting fractures, obstetrics, vivax malaria, amoeba, sting ray envenomation, bullet ant stings, piranha bites, or x-ray technology.

The closest I ever got to x-ray machines was writing an order for a chest x ray. Two or three days later I opened a printed report containing the results of the x-ray findings. Sometimes I would visit the radiology department in my hospital, carrying a large jacket of x-ray films into a radiologist's office, and he would snap the films onto the viewing box and explain to me the shadows and lucencies.

The clinic building at Lomalinda was large with one long hallway. First in the hallway were a couple of rooms for patients staying overnight. Other rooms included a pharmacy, laboratory, nurses and doctor's offices, exam rooms, and a small x-ray room.

Joanne introduced me to the WW II field x-ray machine. She gave me one short tutorial on the technical variables one applies to shoot an x-ray appropriate to the part of the body being imaged. She then took me into the dark room and explained the developing solutions and the two plastic bins the films soak in sequentially.

After that, I was the one flailing in the deep water. I set up the machine, took the x-ray and developed the films, even though Joanne had been acting as expert x-ray technician for years. Being a military issue machine, it was appropriate to be used to image military subjects. One morning a contingent of Colombian soldiers brought in a wounded comrade. I applied the skills taught by Nurse Forsberg to x-ray a Colombian soldier's ankle, after he received shrapnel during an ambush by a group of leftist guerrillas.

Courtesy WW2 US Medical Research Centre (www.med-dept.com)

At Lomalinda I worked alongside the broader therapeutic partnership of a caring community in providing medical care.

Our transportation at Lomalinda was via aging Honda 90 motorcycles. We rode those cycles on the narrow, rutted dirt roads that snaked up and down the hills connecting all the homes and community buildings.

It was after 5 PM when the first phone call came into our home: "Mr. Gallan had an accident, and he is driving himself home on his *moto*."
Two minutes later: "I wanted to tell you that Mr. Gallan just drove by on his *moto* and he is bleeding."
From further along Mr. Gallan's homeward path another concerned caller rang our house: "Mr. Gallan was in some sort of an accident, and he is driving his *moto* and I saw blood on his face."

Mr. Gallan was an outlier among the young, robust Lomalinda denizens. He was a small, frail-appearing 70-year-old man, who spoke with a quiet Southern drawl. He would be the last person to draw attention to himself, hence his nonchalant ride home with his face streaming blood. Our house was on his path home, and I stepped outside to see Mr. Gallan drive by. He smiled and waved politely to me.

I walked to Mr. Gallan's house and saw that he had sustained multiple facial lacerations from a fall off his Honda 90. I called Joanne Forsberg and said that we needed to open the clinic so that I could suture Mr. Gallan.

We transported Mr. Gallan to the clinic, and for the next couple hours, I was privileged to be a participant in a spontaneous community effort of "being the medicine" to Mr. Gallan.

Among the facial lacerations, the most complicated involved his nose. Joanne assembled the various sized suture materials and instruments. Also assembling were other members of the therapeutic team. Concerned nurses and other community members that heard about the accident quietly filed into the clinic.

As I started to approach the challenge of re-approximating the jagged edges, I was acutely aware that this was a man's face I was repairing. I was not a plastic surgeon. My work would create the scars he would be carrying for the rest of his life. Sweat was dripping off my nose from the stress of the task and the tropical heat. Between snipping the ends of my completed sutures, Joanne was moping my brow. Night comes quickly in the tropics. Dusk is fleeting and by 6 PM it is dark. Someone else was holding a flashlight and directing light on the wound. Outside the door of the exam room a small group of folks were praying for Mr. Gallan and the medical crew.

Proof that the repair was a success was that Mrs. Gallan still recognized him when he got home that evening.

Daunting Doors

Doctors can walk the hallways of a hospital as recognized royalty. However, there was one department that always humbled me, when I pushed the swinging doors into that intimidating suite: the ICU, Intensive Care Unit. As a run-of-the-mill family doctor, I entered a world of heart monitors, buzzers, alerts, IV lines, ventilators, and tubes all connected to my patients whose life-threatening illnesses landed them there. The patient charts were thick notebooks tallying all kinds of fluids, temperatures, weights, oxygen saturations, blood values, cultures, x-ray reports; all of which seemed to change by the hour.

The ICU nurses who thrived in those perilous environs wisely and diplomatically coached me as I attempted to punch above my weight. They accompanied me into the patient's room, interpreted the patient's numbers, bringing my attention to the truly salient ones. Before I would write any orders, I would hypothesize them verbally with the nurses, and those experts would graciously modify my orders for the health of the patient.

Chapter Five
"TOM SAID, 'I THINK WE LOVED EACH OTHER TOO MUCH.'"

There is a unique office visit that occurs only once during the doctor's relationship with a patient. It is that first office visit with the surviving spouse after their loved one's death.

All I do is quietly express my sorrow over the loss of their loved one. What follows is ten to fifteen minutes of private, personal remembrance of a spouse, which I, as the only listener, am privileged to receive. Through tears, I am ushered into a grieving but wistful expression of gratitude for the husband or wife who shared their life.

Tom and Ellen were married 57 years. Tom and Ellen came in together for office visits, each with their own cane and their own group of chronic diseases. Tom's ailments were more progressed and accelerating rapidly. He would sit in the right chair while Ellen, in the corner chair, would fuss over his different complaints. Tom's peaceful resignation was a foil to Ellen's concern.

Tom was a retired school principal. His trademark was that he wore a different tie for each day of the school year. Ellen made each one of them. Knowing my clothing signature is also a tie, Ellen sewed a beautiful tie for me a couple years ago.

Today Ellen recounts Tom's courageous battle with his debilitating illnesses. She reflects on his steady, cheerful personality and their lives together. Now with Tom gone, Ted, their son, has stepped in to accompany her in these new, gray days. But not all gray—Ted and Ellen are going to a Pittsburgh Penguins game – a first for Ellen and a bucket-list thrill.

But as I listen to Ellen, I can almost see the large hole in her life. Death has amputated that part of Ellen that was her husband. In the same way that one feels phantom pains from a missing limb, Ellen feels the phantom pains from a missing husband.

I treasure Ellen's gift to me today.

Chapter Six
A COMPLEMENT OF MISTAKEN IDENTITY

My most prized complement from a patient has been when I was the victim of mistaken identity. On a few occasions an older patient has thanked me, addressing me as "Father," confusing me with their priest. If my care has reminded them of the compassionate ministry of their priest, then I am happy to be misidentified with that class of caring professionals.

Compassion:

Is completely missing from every clinical guideline. Needs no insurance approval.

Has no side effects.
Can be universally applied.

But compassion does exact a cost from the giver. Maybe that is why it is so dear to the recipient.

Chapter Seven
TREATING AND HEALING

The doctor's calling is to treat. We treat diseases. We treat people with diseases. We prevent diseases. Ideally, we try to cure diseases. We are much more skilled and successful in treating than in curing. Those patients whose diseases we don't cure become the focus of chronic medical care.

Treating involves practicing evidence-based medicine. The Johns Hopkins Division of General Internal Medicine defines Evidence Based Medicine and how health practitioners apply it:

"Evidence-based medicine is the integration of best research evidence with clinical expertise and patient values. Evidence-based medicine is an interdisciplinary approach which uses techniques from science, engineering, biostatistics, and epidemiology, such as meta-analysis, decision analysis, risk-benefit analysis, and randomized controlled trials to deliver the right care at the right time to the right patient."[9]

Medicine is also traditionally considered a healing profession. Treating versus healing: Is there a difference? Thomas Egnew, in "The Meaning of Healing: Transcending Suffering," Annals of Family Medicine, May/June 2005 states:

"Physicians, trained as biomedical scientists, have focused on the diagnosis, treatment, and prevention of disease. In the process, cure, not care, became the primary purpose of medicine, and the physician's role became 'curer of disease' rather than 'healer of the sick.'"

Egnew defines healing as being "associated with themes of wholeness, narrative, and spirituality. Healing is an intensely personal, subjective experience involving a reconciliation of the meaning an individual ascribes to distressing events with his or her perception of wholeness as a person."[10]

The provider's skills in addressing the personal, subjective issues needed to provide healing are distinct from those used in applying biomedical data to a disease the patient brings into the exam room. Primary care for patients with chronic diseases involves a long-term commitment. In time, with the progression of chronic diseases, there are diminishing returns on the treating side and more opportunities on the healing side. As a healer, I use skills that are not exclusively in a doctor's domain. I borrow tools that are used by healers of all stripes.

Healing Through Listening

The person who is "listening" to their spouse while reading the newspaper, is akin to the provider "listening" to their patient while keyboarding and clicking boxes on their EMR tablet.

Focused, attentive listening is so difficult to do. Providers face escalating, complex documentation pressure. Reimbursement is tied directly to accurate and comprehensive electronic documentation. Focused, attentive listening means that I restrain myself from correcting misinformation, holding back my informed answers that clamor in my brain to be expressed and enlighten the patient. Focused, attentive listening battles the time constraints, as precious seconds tick by when the patient tells you something you heard the last two office visits. Focused, attentive listening mutes my thoughts about the failing stock market, my child's school disaster, or my NCAA bracket collapse.

Full-faced, undistracted listening is a powerful healing gift. That is why Simone Weil says,

"Attention is the rarest and purest form of generosity."

Healing Through Words

Communication between patient and physician is basic to medical care. We listen and we speak. Spoken words that heal are words of encouragement, affirmation, affection, and cheer.

Pleasant words are a honeycomb, sweet to the soul and healing to the bones. Proverbs 16:24

The tongue that brings healing is a tree of life. Proverbs 15:4

Reckless words pierce like a sword, but the tongue of the wise brings healing. Proverbs 12:18

He who answers before listening—that is his folly and his shame. Proverbs 18:13

A word aptly spoken is like apples of gold in a setting of silver. Proverbs 25:11

Aptly spoken words are gamma-knife precise and effective. Aptly spoken words follow focused, attentive listening. Speak words of encouragement, words of affirmation. You can even dispense funny words.

Healing through Laughter

The famous wise man, Groucho Marx, said, "A clown is like an aspirin, only he works twice as fast."

Another famous wise man, Solomon, said "A cheerful heart is good medicine, but a crushed spirit dries up the bones." Prov 17:22

Laughter heals. Laughter is good for us. Multiple studies have shown that laughter improves our hearts, our immune system, lowers blood sugar in people with diabetes, lowers the body's stress hormones, and increases our endorphins, the natural pain killers of our bodies.

A University of Maryland Medical Center in Baltimore study found that people with heart disease were 40% less likely to laugh in a variety of situations compared to people of the same age without heart disease. The 150 people with coronary artery disease laughed less, even in positive situations. They had more anger and hostility than the 150 people without heart disease.[11]

Compare the side effects of the cholesterol-lowering statin drugs with the side effects of laughter. Both can be used as primary and secondary prevention of heart disease. While I wince when patients bring in drug insert papers highlighted with all their side effects, I know of only one proven side effect of laughter: increased facial laugh lines, and, for that, there is always Botox.

Most of us are not professional comedians. But all of us enjoy laughing. Og Mandino, motivational writer and speaker, describes healing laughter in its therapeutic role:

"Laugh at yourself and at life. Not in the spirit of derision or whining self-pity, but as a remedy a miracle drug, that will ease your pain, cure your depression, and help you to put in perspective that seemingly terrible defeat... Never take yourself too seriously."

"I now consider it a good day when I don't step on my boobs." Joan Rivers

I treat the disease seriously, while I treat the person with humor. As a trusted physician, I must exude a confidence of authority by applying evidence-based medicine in treating my patients. At the same time, I must admit the limitations of modern medicine and bring all my healing armamentarium with personal compassion. One without the other is deficient medicine.

Chapter Eight
WATCH THESE MEDICAL PROVIDERS IN ACTION

I typically do not watch "doctor" shows. However, I have identified three short clips that illustrate medical providers being the healing medicine to their patients.

Chief O'Brien, Navy Corpsman in "Captain Phillips"

"Sir, I need you to breathe." "It's going to be OK." "You're safe now."

Chief O'Brien (Danielle Albert) calmly repeated these medicinal phrases to an emotionally and physically traumatized Captain Phillips (Tom Hanks). At the end of the film, which graphically portrayed Phillips' harrowing abduction, when his container vessel is captured by Somali pirates, a bloodied, trembling Phillips is led into O'Brien's exam room. The brief scene captures O'Brien meting out soothing, compassionate care. She clinically describes the 4-centimeter laceration on Phillips' scalp, while continuing to redirect his focus, when he tremors into breakdown.

Danielle Albert, a Navy Corpsman, played Chief O'Brien in the movie "Captain Phillips". Albert was a Sea Cadet with Fort Spokane Battalion Sea Cadets and was serving aboard USS Truxtun (DDG 103) during the filming of the movie.

Watch the scene here:

https://www.youtube.com/watch?v=IJMDdT24_98

Dr. Martin Bettes In
"As Good as it Gets"

Dr. Martin Bettes (Harold Ramis) makes a house call on Spencer, Mrs. Connelly's son, who has debilitating asthma. I am impressed with his matter-of-fact care. He humbly solves the chronic medical problem that has been oppressing the worried, helpless mother.

The ability to remove worry and fear and extend peace and comfort to a person is beautifully portrayed. When Carol Connelly (Helen Hunt) proclaims him as "Doc," I think she imbues that title with the ideals of goodness and capability—the ideals that attracted me to this profession.

Watch the scene here:

https://www.youtube.com/watch?v=cGbhI11K6TU

Suzanne M. Cole, Oncologist
In
"Cancer: The Emperor of All Maladies"

There is no glamour in treating chronic, debilitating, terminal diseases. My medical care cures precious few patients. My roster consists of aging people whose chronic diseases cause increasing pain and debilitation, which they accommodate with varying degrees of resignation, fear, anger, and graciousness. At each quarterly follow-up appointment, I have no breakthrough miracle cure for their osteoarthritis, their dementia, their chronic obstructive pulmonary disease. I can only offer them myself, a consultant, an ally, an empathetic ear and heart.

The powerful clip of Dr. Cole's encounter with a patient who is facing the end of his fight against cancer is difficult to watch. She is the ultimate medicine for the patient. She delivers it, not in an IV, but with the touch of her hand and the invisible care in her voice and presence.

Watch the scene here:

https://www.wvpublic.org/news/2015-03-26/camc-doctor-featured-in-ken-burns-cancer- documentary

You will be enriched in every way so that you can be generous on every occasion, and …your generosity will result in thanksgiving to God. 2 Corinthians 9:11

Chapter Nine
CONCLUSION

Joseph S. Alpert, MD, Editor in Chief of "The American Journal of Medicine", in his article, "The Most Important Qualities for the Good Doctor," opined that "the most important feature of a good doctor was kindness closely allied with empathy." "Sheer knowledge alone without a hefty dose of kindness and empathy, major elements of our humanity, will mean that the 'kindness and empathy-deficient' doctor will not be able to understand what the patient is experiencing and will also not be able to forge a strong and caring relationship with that patient."[12]

The authors in the "Washington Post" article, "For Patients, a Caregiver's Compassion is Essential," give credence to Dr. Alpert's assertion. The article relates the personal experience of Dr. Edward Viner, former chief of the Department of Medicine at Cooper University Health Care. Dr. Viner's as a patient in a hospital ICU:

"It was the nurses he calls his "angels." But not *all* his nurses. When it was time for shift change in the ICU, Viner says he felt he could detect almost immediately if the nurse coming on duty truly cared. He could tell some nurses cared deeply, but some did not.

'When my nurses cared,' he distinctly remembers, 'I knew that shift would be a positive experience and that their compassion would help me fight on and help save me.'"[13]

Listening, empathizing, laughing, and affirming is how we heal, care for, and "save" our patients. There is a quote by Allison Massari, healthcare keynote speaker, which crystalizes the vital importance of the provider as a person in medical care:

"The power of what you do goes far beyond the technical part of your job. You are healing the places medicine cannot touch. In fact, YOU are the medicine."[14]

I embarked on a path that has enriched my life, by affording me profound personal relationships. How can I be anything but thankful for that opportunity? This is my expression of thanks to God and to all those He placed in my life to enrich me.

Notes

Chapter 1 Introduction

1. Institute of Medicine, Committee on the Future of Primary Care, Donaldson MS, et al. Primary Care: America's Health in a New Era. National Academy Press; 1996.

Chapter 2 One Friday in May

2. legacy patients, so-called, because their long-term use of often high-dose opioid or stimulant therapy is a legacy of past, more aggressive prescribing practices.
3. "First, do no harm" or primum non nocere, is attributed to the ancient Greek physician Hippocrates. It isn't a part of the Hippocratic Oath. It is from another of his works called Of the Epidemics.

Chapter 3 Vitamin E – Encouragement

4. "First do no harm" Hippocrates

Chapter 4 Physician-Nurse Partnership

5. Bor, R. Gill, S. Miller, R. & Evans, Counselling in Health Care Settings (United Kingdom: Palgrave Macmillan, 2009) 56.
6. Baiyekusi I. Physician-nurse relationship: Nurses' perception in internal medicine and surgical units. 2009; oai: www.theseus.fi:10024/24852.
7. Kramer M, Schmalenberg C. Securing good nurse-physician relationships: Explore the link between collaboration and quality patient care. Nursing Management 2003;7, 34-38.
8. Kramer M, Schmalenberg C. Nurse-Physician Relationships in Hospitals: 20, 000 Nurses Tell Their Story. Critical Care Nurse 2009;29 (1), 74-83.

Chapter 7 Treating and Healing

9. "Evidence-Based Medicine." Div. Gen. Internal Medicine. Johns Hopkins Medicine.
   https://www.hopkinsmedicine.org/gim/research/method/ebm.html
10. Egnew TR. The meaning of healing: transcending suffering. Ann. Fam. Med. 2005;3(3):255-262.

11. Miller M, Fry WF. The effect of mirthful laughter on the human cardiovascular system. Medical Hypotheses. 2009;73(5): 636-639.

Chapter 9 Conclusion

12. Alpert JS. The Most Important Qualities for the Good Doctor. Am. J. Med. 2021;134(7):825-826.
13. Trzeciak S, Mazzarelli A. (2019, May 14). For patients, a caregiver's compassion is essential. The Washington Post, p. E3.
14. https://allisonmassari.com/healthcare-keynote-speaker

ABOUT THE AUTHOR

David Clifford grew up in the suburbs of Philadelphia. He moved to Warren, PA to start practicing family medicine and, along with his wife, Diane, raise three wonderful children. Other than serving as a doctor with Wycliffe Bible Translators for seven years, his entire medical career was in Warren. He loves wildflowers, still jogs on gimpy knees and is guilty of laughing unashamedly at his own antics. He and Diane now reside in Horsham, PA.

Made in the USA
Middletown, DE
28 July 2023